LEVEL 5

Written by: Coleen Degnan-Veness
Series Editor: Melanie Williams

Pearson Education Limited
Edinburgh Gate, Harlow,
Essex CM20 2JE, England
and Associated Companies throughout the world.

ISBN: 978-1-4082-8844-3

This edition first published by Pearson Education Ltd 2014

11 13 15 17 19 20 18 16 14 12

Set in 15/19pt OT Fiendstar
Printed in Great Britain by Ashford Colour Press Ltd.
SWTC/02

Illustrations: Phil Littler

For a complete list of the titles available in the Pearson English Kids Readers series, please go to
www.pearsonenglishkidsreaders.com. Alternatively, write to your local Pearson Education office or to
Pearson English Readers Marketing Department, Pearson Education, Edinburgh Gate, Harlow, Essex CM20 2JE, England.

Ice Island is the coldest place on Earth. About fifty people live in the only town called Ice Town. Polar bears are the only animals on the island.

One Monday, the explorer Jason Strong got a phone call from Ice Town.

"Can you come quickly?" the police officer asked. "There are large tracks everywhere. They look like yeti tracks. People are really afraid."

Jason arrived that evening. On Tuesday afternoon, he found tracks.

I'll text Megan and Greg for help!

On Wednesday morning, Jason's young cousins, Megan and Greg, arrived by boat. Jason met them.

"We all know that yetis are a mystery," he said. "Their tracks look like this, I believe." He showed them a picture.

"What big feet!" said Megan.

"Now, look at *this* photo on my cell phone," said Jason. "I took it ten minutes ago."

"They look nearly the same!" Greg said.

"B ... b ... b ... but ... can there be a yeti on Ice Island?" Megan asked.

"Maybe," said Jason. "We have to find out. Let's go to the Monitoring Station in the southwest of the island. I'll show you a map of Ice Island and we'll make plans for tracking the yeti. Climb into the helicopter."

The children were excited! They jumped into Jason's helicopter. WHOOOSH!

"Look!" shouted Megan. "More tracks!"

Greg looked out of the window. "Those tracks are very strange and very BIG!"

From above, Ice Island looked small in the big ocean.

In the Monitoring Station, Jason sat down in front of one of the computers.

"First, I want to show you some more photos. I took them earlier this morning," he said.

Suddenly, Greg said, "Look! There's a poster on one of those trees in this photo."

WANTED

FOR STEALING POLAR BEARS!

Doctor Danger and Hopeless Harry
Help us capture them

"Do you think those men are on Ice Island?" Megan asked.

"It's possible," said Greg. "We'll keep our eyes open."

Later, Jason's friend Pandora Parris arrived at the Monitoring Station.

"Pandora's a scientist," Jason told Greg and Megan. "She's going to help us track the yeti for two or three days."

"Jason, do you have enough skis for all of us?" Pandora asked.

"No, I don't. Can you take Megan and Greg to Ice Town? Here's some money."

"Great idea! We'd like to see Ice Town," said Greg.

"Follow me!" said Pandora.

Pandora, Megan, and Greg walked by a lake toward Ice Town.
Suddenly, Greg shouted. "Look at that!"

In the center of the lake, there was a beautiful ice sculpture of a whale's tail.

"I love that sculpture," said Pandora.

"Does it ever melt?" asked Megan.

"No, never," Pandora answered. "Ice never melts on Ice Island!"

"Never?" asked Greg.

"Never. And the people of Ice Town don't *want* warmer temperatures here. They don't want glaciers to melt and flood their town."

The next morning, the explorers were ready to start tracking.

"Look! Polar bear tracks!" said Greg.

"That's strange. Polar bears never come near the Monitoring Station," Jason said.

"Very strange," said Pandora. "Maybe it was in danger."

"Maybe a yeti frightened it," Megan said.

"Let's go," said Jason. "Megan and Pandora, go east to the forest. Greg, we'll go north. Maybe yetis are dangerous so be careful. Oh, and if you see Doctor Danger or Hopeless Harry, call the police."

Jason and Greg skied north toward some caves.
Suddenly, Greg stopped and pointed. "Look! Tracks!"

"They're polar bear tracks," said Jason.

"Yes, I know. But look over there! Those tracks are new.
They're not from animals or skis."

"You're right," said Jason. "Who's
driving out here?"

"Maybe other trackers are here and they're
looking for the yeti, too," said Greg.

"Trackers ski or walk. They don't drive," said Jason.

"Doctor Danger and Hopeless Harry are somewhere
near here," Greg thought.

When Pandora and Megan were near the forest, Megan began to feel nervous. She looked afraid. Pandora had an idea.

"Let's stop," said Pandora. "I just remembered a joke that you'll like."

"Where can you find an ocean without any water?" Pandora asked.

Megan thought for a minute. "I don't know. Where?" she asked.

"On a map!" answered Pandora.

Megan smiled. "Very funny," she said.

They did not see the young yeti in the tree who loved Pandora's joke!

Later, Jason and Greg skied near the lake.

"We were here yesterday with Pandora," said Greg.

"Did you see the ice sculpture?" asked Jason.

"Yes. The Whale's Tail is beautiful."

Suddenly, Greg shouted, "Look! The Whale's Tail is melting!"

"What? That's impossible!" said Jason.

They skied nearer. It was true. The Whale's Tail *was* melting!

"We have to do something or Ice Town will flood!" said Jason.

Jason took a machine from his pocket and read the temperature.

"*What* is happening?" he cried. "It's getting warmer! I can see it go up! Look!"

Greg looked. "You're right. Ice Town is in great danger," he said.

"We must do something *quickly* or the glacier will melt in twenty four hours!" said Jason.

"Why is the air getting warmer?" asked Greg.

"I really do not know," said Jason.

In the forest, two men stood next to a cage with three angry polar bears inside.

Doctor Danger shouted at Harry. "Where's that other female bear?"

"She ran when I opened the cage," said Harry.

"Zoos pay a lot of money for females!" said Doctor Danger.

"But we still have one female and two males. We'll be rich!" said Harry.

Behind some trees, Pandora and Megan listened.

"I know those faces! They were on the poster!" said Megan.

Doctor Danger turned and saw Pandora and Megan behind a tree.

"Who's there?" he shouted.

"We are," said Pandora angrily. "We heard every word. We're going to stop you!"

"You can't stop us!" said Hopeless Harry.

"Let's go, Harry," said Doctor Danger.

They drove away very quickly through the forest. Pandora and Megan tried to catch them but they could not.

"They'll come back for the polar bears and then we'll get them," said Pandora.

On Thursday evening in the Monitoring Station, Jason turned on the computers.

"There are cameras on Ice Island so we can see everything everywhere," he said.

But it was a dark night so Jason could not find the thieves.

"I'll look again in the morning," he said.

After the children went to bed, Jason and Pandora talked for hours about the thieves *and* the temperature.

That night, Megan dreamed that she found a key inside a cave.

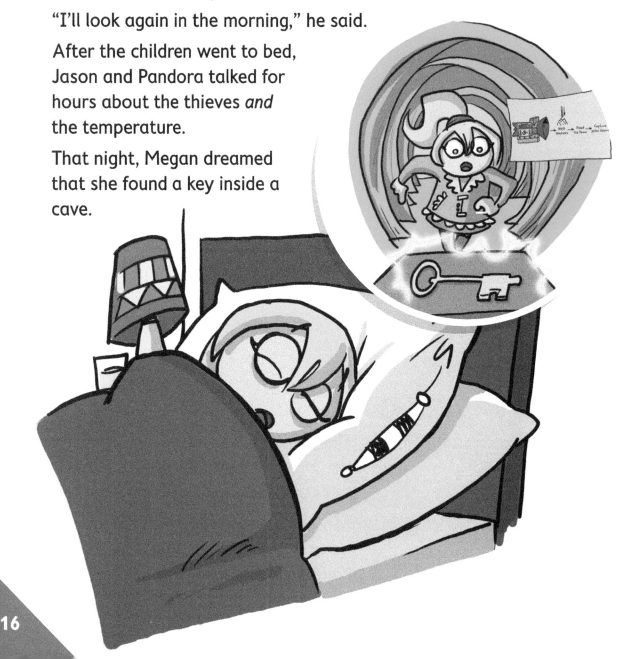

When Megan woke up early the next morning, she knocked on Greg's bedroom door. She had to tell him about her dream.

"We *must* go to the caves!" said Megan.

Quickly, they put on their skis and went north to the caves. Inside the largest cave, on a table, was a key.

"I think Doctor Danger and Hopeless Harry have a machine that melts glaciers," said Greg. "*That* explains why the sculpture is melting!"

"Why do they want to flood Ice Town?" Megan asked.

"Maybe they want to be the only people on Ice Island," said Greg. "Then no one can stop them capturing polar bears."

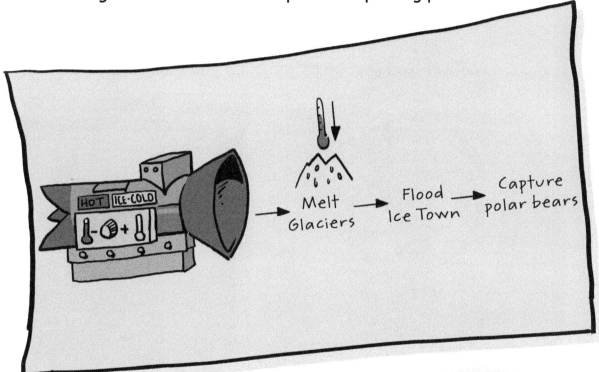

Three yetis in the next cave listened. They did not like what they heard.

"We have to find their machine! I must text Jason!" said Megan.

Ten minutes later, Jason arrived.

"Pandora will be here soon," said Jason.
"She's bringing another scientist."

Megan and Greg showed Jason the key and the plan.
When Jason saw the plan, his face went white.

"Everything on Ice Island will die!" Jason said.

"We need to stop them!" said Megan.

"We must find their machine!" said Greg.

The three yetis were not far away. They heard
everything.

Pandora and the scientist arrived by helicopter.

"This is Milo Moon," said Pandora. "He knows everything about glaciers and polar bears."

"Polar bears find food under the ice," said Milo. "No ice means less food."

"Hungry polar bears' lives are in danger," said Pandora.

"We found a key and a plan inside a cave this morning," said Megan.

"We think that Doctor Danger and Hopeless Harry have a machine that melts glaciers," said Greg.

"We must find it!" said Milo.

Suddenly, they heard a terrible noise!

CR...AAAAA...CK!

"What was that?" shouted Megan.

"It's the glacier!" cried Pandora.

"It's breaking and moving!"

"We *must* find those thieves and their machine!" said Milo. "We don't have much time!"

"And we must open the cage with this key so the polar bears can get out!" said Megan.

"That's right. We have to save those bears!" said Jason.

"Let's go!" said Megan.

In the forest, Megan pointed, "Over there is the thieves' tent. And *there* is the cage."

"Give me the key. I'll open it!" said Jason.

"But those hungry bears will eat us!" said Megan nervously.

"Milo has a dart gun," Pandora explained. "It makes the polar bears sleep. Then he'll put the bears inside a big net and pull them up into the helicopter."

"I'll take them to a colder place on the island," said Milo.

"Good!" said Megan.

They skied toward the polar bears' cage. Megan gave the key to Jason. Milo had his dart gun and net ready.

Suddenly, Doctor Danger and Hopeless Harry arrived.

"They look angry," said Greg. "Maybe they went to the cave."

Doctor Danger shouted at Harry, "Did you lose the key?"

"No!" said Harry.

"Where's the plan?"

"It was there last night! You saw it!" said Harry.

"We took it!" shouted Megan.

Doctor Danger turned and saw Megan and her friends.

"Where's the machine?" shouted Greg.

"What machine?" asked Harry.

"Tell us or we'll put you in that cage with the polar bears!" said Milo.

Doctor Danger was afraid of Milo's gun. He said, "Behind that cage is a door to an underground tunnel that goes through the glacier. Our machine's inside it."

"Does it change the island's temperature?" asked Megan.

Harry smiled.

You wanted the island for your business! But now you can forget about selling polar bears to zoos!

"I'll put these thieves in that empty cage," Milo said. "You four *must* find that machine!"

Jason, Pandora, Megan, and Greg quickly found the door to the tunnel and went underground.

Milo opened the cage and pushed the thieves inside. He ran toward the polar bear cage with his dart gun and net, but he did not see the rock on the ground in front of him.

Suddenly, Milo fell over it and hit his head! He did not move.

"Ha!" laughed Doctor Danger. "I have another key for this cage in my pocket! He isn't going to wake up very soon! Let's go!"

Doctor Danger opened the cage. The thieves ran.

A yeti behind some large trees put out his foot and Harry fell on to Milo's net. Doctor Danger fell over Harry. They never saw the yeti. They did not know what happened! When they tried to get up, they could not get out of the net.

The children ran quickly through the tunnel. Pandora and Jason followed.

"There's water everywhere," said Pandora. "The glacier is melting fast!"

"We don't have much time!" Jason shouted.

At the end of the tunnel, the children found the machine!

"Oh, no. It's on HOT!" Greg shouted.

"Quick" said Megan. "Change it!"

Greg put out his hand to change it when the ice under his feet broke. He started to fall.

Quickly, Pandora caught him. Megan changed it to ICE-COLD!

They ran back through the tunnel and found Milo inside his helicopter. On the ground, inside the net, the polar bears slept.

Megan shouted at the thieves, "You capture polar bears because you want to sell them to zoos! Who's laughing now?"

Don't put us in the helicopter with the bears ... pleeeease!

Why not? They're hungry!

Pandora thought of another joke.

"What did the polar bear *eat* after the dentist pulled out its tooth?" Pandora asked.

"The dentist!" shouted Megan.

Then another helicopter arrived.

"We're happy to see you!" said Greg.

"We left as soon as you called," said one police officer. "We want Doctor Danger and Hopeless Harry to spend many years inside a cage!"

"Throw away the key!" said Greg. "They're never going anywhere!"

The other police officer said, "Thank you for capturing them!"

They took Doctor Danger and Hopeless Harry and flew away.

"I'm taking these bears to a colder place. They'll wake up soon," said Milo.

"We saved Ice Town and the polar bears," said Pandora.

"That *was* an adventure!" said Megan.

"Let's track that yeti!" said Jason.

"Let's go to the lake!" said Megan.

"We can have a party near the Whale's Tail!" said Greg.

"Maybe Doctor Danger hoped to capture the yeti, too," said Pandora. "Not one zoo in the world has a yeti."

"Not yet," Jason said. "And I hope that they never will!"

Three yetis high up in the trees smiled.

Activity page ❶

Before You Read

❶ Look at the picture from page 6 and answer the questions.

   a How many people are there?

   b Where do you think they are?

   c What are they looking at on the computer?

   d Who are the men on the WANTED poster, do you think?

❷ Find the words below in your dictionary. Look at the pictures on pages 3, 5, 6, 8, 10, 14, 22, and 27. On which page can you see these things?

a tracks	**b** polar bears
c a helicopter	**d** a poster
e skis	**f** a sculpture
g a cage	**h** a dart gun
i a net	**j** a machine

Activity page ❷

After You Read

❶ Who in the story ...

a are explorers?

b have their photos on a Wanted Poster?

c are scientists?

d loves the Whale's Tail sculpture?

e takes the key from the cave and why?

❷ Read and write True (T) or False (F).

a Polar bears often go near the Monitoring Station. ☐

b Trackers ski or walk. They do not drive. ☐

c When Jason reads the temperature, he feels happier. ☐

d Doctor Danger and Hopeless Harry sell polar bears to zoos. ☐

e Megan and Pandora find the thieves' plan in the cave. ☐

f Pandora and Milo Moon arrive at the forest by boat. ☐

g Milo's dart gun makes the polar bears sleep. ☐

h Doctor Danger and Hopeless Harry's machine can melt the glacier. ☐

❸ Draw the map of Ice Island with the lake in the center. On the map, label ...

a the Monitoring Station

b the Whale's Tail ice sculpture

c the forest

d the cave

e the ocean